EXQUISITE
FLOWERS

COLOR. DREAM. CREATE.

VIRGINIE GUYARD

BLACK DOG
& LEVENTHAL
PUBLISHERS
NEW YORK

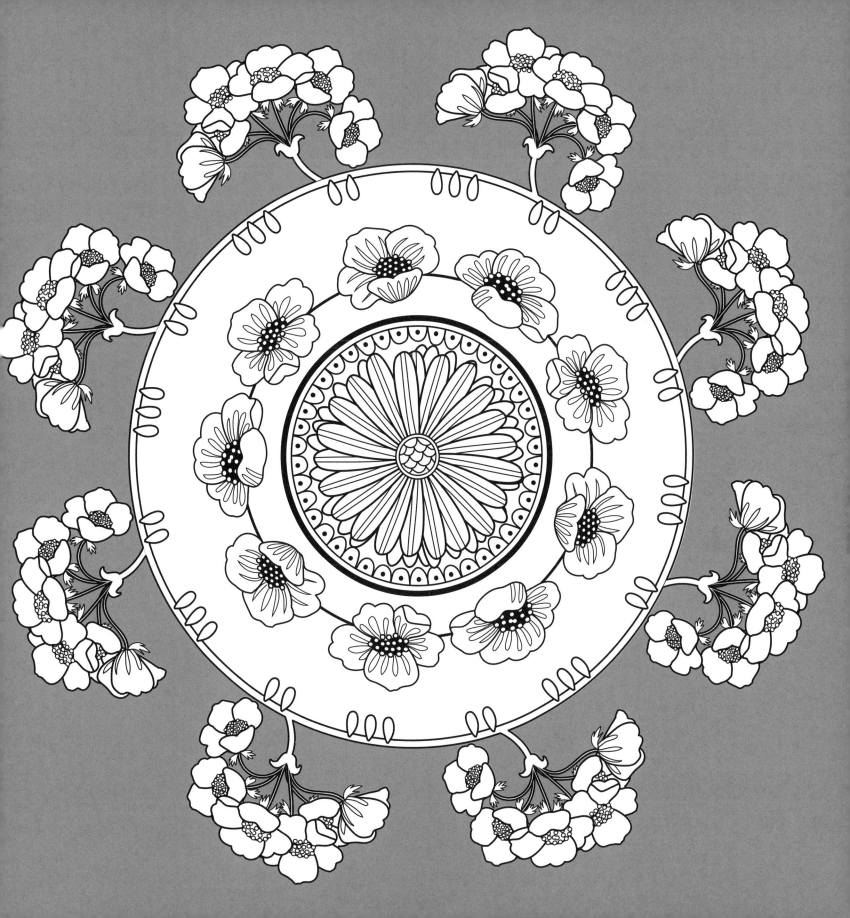

Published originally under the title "Fleurs exquises"
© 2015 by Editions Solar, Paris
English translation copyright: © 2016 by Black Dog & Leventhal Publishers.

Black Dog & Leventhal Publishers
Hachette Book Group
1290 Avenue of the Americas
New York, NY 10104

www.hachettebookgroup.com
www.blackdogandleventhal.com

Printed in China

Cover and interior design by Virginia Arraga de Malherbe

IM

First Edition: March 2016
10 9 8 7 6 5 4 3 2 1

Black Dog & Leventhal Publishers is an imprint of Hachette Books, a division of Hachette Book Group.
The Black Dog & Leventhal Publishers name and logo are trademarks of Hachette Book Group, Inc.

The Hachette Speakers Bureau provides a wide range of authors for speaking events.
To find out more, go to www.HachetteSpeakersBureau.com or call (866) 376-6591.

The publisher is not responsible for websites (or their content) that are not owned by the publisher.

Library of Congress Cataloging-in-Publication Data available upon request.

ISBN: 978-0-316-31259-2